I Am Not A Poet

Journeys In Faith And Self-Discovery

Jackie David Johns

ISBN: 061557064X
ISBN-13: 978-0615570648

DEDICATION

To Cheryl, my partner in life and ministry.
I searched and found my pearl of great price.
She is my companion, friend, counselor and guide.

CONTENTS

"The Lane"
O'Quinn Home Place
Charlton County, Georgia

PREFACE

The "poems" in this volume were composed over a period of more than twenty years. Most were not written to be read by others. They were instead exercises in self-discovery. I began writing them at a point of great despair. My faith was under tremendous strain. Everything I thought I knew about God and myself was being challenged at the core of my being. I thought I had been faithful. I was doing my part, but God wasn't doing His, or so it seemed. Like Jacob long ago, I was wrestling with God and God was winning.

Out of those experiences, I discovered some truths about myself, my God, and the Christian life. First, knowing God requires that we also know ourselves. The journey toward God always begins with a journey inward. Before we can embrace the One who is wholly other, we must embrace and discard those traits that cannot exist in His presence. All that can be shaken must be shaken until only that which is everlasting remains (Hebrews 12: 27).

Humility is both the starting point and the necessary posture for any relationship with God. He resists the proud but gives grace to the humble (James 4:6, I Peter 5:5). I have learned that humility is less about our thoughts and more about the inclinations of our heart. One can rightly understand one's place within a race of depraved creatures and at the same time maintain a prideful spirit, the tendency to see oneself as the best of the least of these. To know one's self is to see one's self before the face of a holy God where there are no excuses. Knowing God requires the deconstruction of the idol we have carved as our self-image.

I had developed a healthy self-image; I knew my strengths and weaknesses. I required a lot of God's help to deconstruct. The writings in this volume are presented not as examples of great truths. They are instead portraits of my processes of deconstruction and reconstruction, presentations of my struggles and discoveries.

Second, I discovered that the soul cannot be known through reason alone. Prose is woefully inadequate to communicate the inner self. The human heart is prone to hide behind rhetoric, carefully constructed defensible explanations of our thoughts. But when it offers itself voluntarily and without reservation, it does so with song -- music, rhythm, rhyme and cadence.

Prose is linear. Life is multidimensional. Prose is mechanical. Life is organic, a dynamic system of multiple organs interacting simultaneously. Prose is a solo without accompaniment. Life is a symphony even when it is a cacophony of discord. At the moment my self-image crumbled I found I could only express my true self in screams and groans and poetic phrases.

Third, there is a human drive to know ourselves in the eyes of others. For most of us the idol of our self-image is constructed for the admiration of people, not God. We project our best self, the self we want to be, as though it is our true self. If others see us as that perfected being, then perhaps we can become that person.

Human relationships are both the fountain of and an obstacle to knowing God. Adam and Eve were created to know each other knowing God. The drive for intimacy with another human is linked to the drive for intimacy with God. We were created to know and to be known as we are known; this is the destiny of all who are in Christ. In this life, it is also the battleground for sin.

Adam and Eve fell into sin when they agreed to share a knowledge apart from their creator. And the knowledge they shared was the knowledge that divided them. In eating the fruit of the tree of the knowledge of good and evil they lost their fellowship with God and their harmony with each other. Ever since that fateful choice, humans hunger to return to the Garden. That hunger is in truth a craving to return to that condition of knowing and being known.

Human relationships are by design a primary mode for knowing God. He is a witness and participant in all relationships. They are a reflection of His very image. It is for this cause that all sins against others are in fact sins against God. Discord in human relationships is caustic to our relationship with God.

Conversely, the struggle to know and be known by others can be an exercise in Godly worship. The altar of our forgiveness and our ministry of reconciliation are merged into a single event (Matthew 5: 23-24). The quest for righteous intimacy is integral to our transformation into the likeness of Christ.

Fourth, I have discovered the journey to our final place in God, that place of unencumbered fellowship with Him, must be fully realized and yet ever forward. We know Him now, and in knowing Him our hunger is to know Him more fully. As I have written elsewhere, orthodoxy, both in the sense of "correct worship" and the sense of "sound doctrine" is our purpose for existence. The glory of God is the port toward which Christians sail and the stream in which we sail. It is our calling and our destiny to worship Him in Spirit and in Truth.

Finally, I have discovered that trials and tests in life are not about demonstrating how much we know or what skills we have gained. They do not come to us as challenges to demonstrate how well we can stand on our own. In the darkest days we are not alone; He is with us. Not only is Christ with us in our tribulations, He is at work in, for, and through us. The trying of our faith is not for the purpose of measuring how much faith we have. No, the furnaces of life exist to temper our faith, to perfect and to strengthen it.

I compiled and edited these poems out of a deep sense of compulsion. In October of this year I felt a strong drive to write

"Into Your Presence" as an expression of my love for God and His Word. When I finished the two stanzas which appear in this volume, the compulsion shifted to a need to revisit my older poems.

As I pulled them out of various files and reviewed them, a thought emerged that I should share them with my children and grand-children (when they are older). I wanted them to know my heart, to see a side of me they might not know, and to know the depths of my faith. The subtitle of this collection could easily have been "Cries of My Heart."

I reasoned that a compiled volume might be a good gift for my siblings as well. While editing the collection with family in mind, I read a few of them to some of my students at the Pentecostal Theological Seminary. The response of some, especially those seasoned in life and ministry, seemed to suggest that these accounts of my struggles with faith might speak to others, let them know they are not alone.

With Cheryl's encouragement, I decided to make these journeys of self-discovery available to the public. Thus, I offer these writings with the hope they will serve as a source of strength in troubling times. I pray my struggles and discoveries offer hope and, above all, that Christ is glorified by the veracity of my efforts, if not the validity of my thoughts.

As exercises in self-discovery, these poems are in a sense autobiographical. A few of them are explicitly narrative in nature, tracing issues through the seasons of my life. Further, except for the first and last pieces, the writings appear in the order in which they were written. That arrangement is in one sense also autobiographical. However, the sequence can be misleading as it does not accurately portray my life over the time frame of these writings.

I began creative writing in a time of great angst. Poetry was a means of processing hurt and disappointment, not joy and contentment. It took some time before I would write for other purposes. The reader should not infer the preponderance of anguish in the early poems implies a total absence of tranquility. The implication is simply that I had not begun to write in times when all was well.

As noted above, these poems were not written for public dissemination. (Although, I have posted a few on my blog.) Most were born out of deeply personal struggles to express how I was experiencing life. I needed to process those inner conflicts of faith. Two were written as instructions for my daughters. Others were written as acts of private worship, attempts to "think God's thoughts after Him."

The one exception to this is the title piece, "I Am Not a Poet." That poem was composed on the occasion of the 2009 Minister's Week at the Pentecostal Theological Seminary. Cheryl was the program director that year and she chose as a theme "Worship and the Arts." I was drafted to read some of my poems. I wrote my opening disclaimer in verse.

I offer my apologies to those accustomed to fine literature. I am not a poet. I am but a fellow traveler who desires to know and to be known. These are the cries of my heart.

The photographs in this volume were selected to honor my ancestors who chose in the early nineteenth century to settle in the southeast corner of Georgia. My grandmother, Irene Nettles Johns, spent her early life on Billy's Island in the Okefenokee Swamp. When her family resettled in Charlton County, her parents became members of the Corinth Primitive Baptist Church. The sloughs, scrub oaks, moss, cypress stumps and pines are etched into my DNA, perhaps with some dreaded Calvinism as well.

Jackie David Johns
Cleveland, Tennessee
November 25, 2011

Bethlehem Cemetery
Brantley County, Georgia

1.

I AM NOT A POET

Poets are artists
Painting on the canvas of our imagination
With words, rhythms, and sounds
Fused into a single medium
Evoking a knowledge from within

Poets are sculptors of the mind
Molding, bending and shaping ideas
Until they serve a greater end
Exposing hidden forms
Forged in our collective consciousness
Framed by common experience

Poets are jewelers
Matching words with emotions
Spinning phrases into golden chains
All linked by mystery more than grammar
Highlighting subtle facets of awareness
Each complementing the other
Valued for the whole and for the part

Poets are musicians
Connecting the tangible
And the eternal
With the melody of angels
Tapping out a cadence
With Syllables and silence
Harmonizing and resonating
In sequential tones of thought

Poets are magicians
Waving syllables and phrases
Before our very eyes
Entertaining us with the ordinary
Set in motion in plain sight
Only to surprise us
With unexpected delight
Words, once dull and listless
Suddenly enlightening
Poised, refined, enchanting

I am not a poet
I lack the wisdom, grace and skill
Not to mention the will
To weave a tapestry
Of our shared humanity
I cannot carve a sculpture of your inner self
Nor paint a portrait of who you long to be

I am not a poet
I am just a collector
A hoarder
And a tinkerer
A gatherer of thoughts and ideas
From time to time
I open the closet of my mind
Allowing all the clutter
To spill out in one big mess
Just so I can pick it up
Arrange the words in rows
Connected like fingers and toes
Flowing down a page
In feigned complexity
Made clear for all to see
Implying some great significance
Yet void of such magnificence

I leave it to the reader
To plumb their deeper meaning
Add whatever intention
You imagined in my conceptions
As for me, I only wanted
To make a connection

April 2009

Okefenokee Swamp
Charlton County, Georgia

2.

WHY?

Like a meteor it streaks across
The cosmos of my mind
Suddenly as focused as
Letters on a neon sign

This question of a single word
Has proved a fickle friend
As a child I tapped its powers
Unaware of its hidden end

Then it was a magic word
Drawing attention from the giants of my land
"Mommy, why are flowers red?"
"Daddy, why are others blue?"

"Teacher, why is milk so white?
Why is it dark at night?
Why are birds in the sky?"
Why?...Why?...Why?

I didn't really care to know
Any answer would do
To show they love me so
And they shared my outward view

Yet in me a light had dawned
It was to their world I belonged
And it was I, a growing child
Who had begun to think

Youth taught me other uses
For this syllable of thought
"Why?" offered a solution
to the world without

"Why" became the key
To the mysteries of the universe
With it I could probe
A world complex, diverse

Set my own pace, seldom deterred
I could seek the truth
Explore the things I saw and heard
Oh, the privileges of youth!

Why are flowers red or blue
Or some other lovely hue?
Why are the grasses green?
There are causes for these things

Mine to have and own
If I sought through reason alone
My friendly word became a guide
With science as its bride

Helping me explore
The wonders of the world
Reaching far beyond myself
For the mysteries of time

I did not yet know my companion
Aimed to rule my life
A master who would drive
Where I would not wish to go

Compelling thoughts I did not want
Demanding answers I preferred forgot
Still I felt the quest my friend
Leading to some greater end

Intimacy added new dimensions
To this growing obsession
There was yet another reality
The truth between you and me

So again I beg it of another
Seeking some response
Only now her words have power
Driving me to thought

Why?...Why?...Why?
Again driven to know
Compelled into this quest
Still hoping for the best

That pretentious little word
Seems my enemy of late
Wanting more than I have to give
Giving more than I can bear to live

"Why?" I only wish I knew
Our truth, our reality
The answers are not in me
Nor even deep in you

They are buried inside of us
To be found if we both desire
For the question is none other than "why?"
"Why us?"

November 1988

Okefenokee Swamp
Charlton County, Georgia

3.

WHO AM I?

I once was confident
Keen with my perceptions
Always holding reservations
Weighing all my options

Now, my confidence is shaken
The ones I knew the best I know the least
Visions of my competence are taken
The ones I lived to serve, I served the least

Who am I
To reach out my hand
As if to strengthen others in this weary land
When it is I who cannot stand?

Who am I
To reach out to others in despair
As if I could provide repair
When I am shackled by all my cares?

Who am I
To think I have insight
As if I had special understanding of the right
When it is I who am void of sight?

Who am I
To offer rest
As if I know what's best
When it was I who failed my test?

I want to help
But who can I help?
I live to serve
I serve to live

Now I lack the nerve
To reach out and give
I have nothing in reserve.
I have nothing left to give

December 1988

4.

TEARS

Glistening drops of liquid gold
Announcing stories begging to be told

Cantankerous, salty little drops
Refusing to come, refusing to stop

Each one a prisoner of my heart
Seeking opportunities to start

Wanting to escape from me
Return to their mother the sea

When I was a little child
My heart was tender and mild

Tears were always there
In touch with my every care

I cried when I had a scrape
And when they removed the bandage tape

I cried when I wanted my way
Begging to go or seeking to stay

I cried when I'd said all I could
Longing to be understood

I cried when I felt rejected
Hungering to be accepted

Tears were always there
As normal as breathing air

Warm, then cold upon my cheek
Freedom from them I could not seek

All I could do was bury my head
Sobbing into the pillow on my bed

Desperately wanting someone to care
Yet strangely content in my solace there

Ashamed of my childish tears
Overwhelmed by inner fears

Then it happened, how, I can't explain
I suddenly knew I could refrain

I took control of my inner strife
Discovered a whole new way of life

When I felt my eyes begin to burn
I held my breath, a simple trick I learned

I assured myself I didn't have to cry
I could hold it in until I die

Before long it wasn't even a fight
I had my emotions bottled tight

Latter I discovered the trauma of being a "man"
Emotions are essential, part of God's plan

I may have locked them in
But what did I really win?

When I stopped my tears and gained control
I closed the windows of my soul

I locked myself inside a cage
Outer peace, inner rage

Only God could set me free
So I gave them all to him, exposed the inner me

Now tears may trickle or come in a flood
They're a part of me, they're in my blood

December 1988

5

LONELY ROADS

There are lonely roads to be traveled
Journeys of solitary subsistence
Dark paths of isolation
Seasons of resistance

Others refuse to come
But the journeys must be made
As much flights of escape
As searches for a better place

These are roads out of despair
Promising a nobler land
Traversing uncharted terrain
With threats of inner pain

Temptations to retreat
or to settle in one place
Invite surrender to defeat
Abandon the hope of grace

February 1989

Okefenokee Swamp
Charlton County, Georgia

6.

WILL YOU HEAR?

Will you hear
my soul crying out
not in anger but in fear
lonely, full of doubt?

Will you hear my words
not just syllables in the wind,
Revelations of my inner self
looking for a friend

Unless my tears
touch your ears,
You cannot know
the torment of my soul.

Will you hear?
Will you have compassion
Let my tears touch your ears
Acknowledge my desperation?

Corinth Primitive Baptist Church
Charlton County, Georgia

7.

WHERE?

Oh, God, where?
Where do I go from here?
I sought to know your will
Want to know it still
All you have said is "wait, be patient"
I've tried to sit and be content
How long am I to linger under this tree
Looking for a messenger of majesty?

Where must I go to hear you speak?
A still, small voice is all I seek

I am an unworthy instrument
Not certain of Your intent
I keep myself at Your feet
Unwilling to consider retreat
Knowing I have nothing to give
Not even the life I live
What I do not possess, I cannot tender
All I can hope is full surrender
Place in your hands
All your will demands
You are Creator God
I a vessel of sod.

Where must I go to hear you speak?
A still, small voice is all I seek

Early 90's

8.

THE HONOR IN OUR NAME

Promises made to be broken
Are better left unspoken

Commitments made in the eyes of God
On this journey that we trod

Shall one day reappear
With smile, or frown, or tear

They will boldly proclaim
The honor in our name

Some full and robust
Will speak as they must

Straight, tall, upright
Glowing in the light

They will tell of our sincerity
Faithfulness, and integrity

Others frail with gloom
As if coming from our tomb

Will recall their abandonment
How forsaken without lament

And speak of our duplicity
Negligence and unreliability

Their power is not to heal
But only to reveal

The honor in our name
Or the ugliness of our shame

Yes, promises made to be broken
Are better left unspoken

November 1992

9.

A PROVERB

Dearest Daughter,

Listen to the words of your father
Righteousness is fulfilled
Not by avoiding evil alone
But by doing good always

For this Christ came
To free us from sin
Not from the penalty alone
But from its control within

Cleansed from our transgressions
Clothed in His righteousness
Recipients of His mercy
Granted grace that we might bless

Honor your father and your mother
That your days may be long
Seek ways to build them up
In their service become strong

Find the good in you
That first flowed from them
Let it shine for all to see
And they will glow more brightly

Add to the wealth of their memories
Your own nuggets of gold
Fuel their hopes for your future
And the future of those to come

Where they have failed
Never fail
Where they have excelled
Soar on the winds of their courage

Know and be true to yourself
Know and be true to them
From them you came
Unto them you will be gathered

August 1996

10.

VIRTUE

Virginity and Virtue
These are not the same

One is a state
The other a trait

One a gift to be cherished
The other a grace to be pursued

One speaks only of our past
The other proclaims our destiny

One may be stolen or forsaken
The other lost by neglect

The virgin, though untouched by human hand
May be soiled by inner desire

The virtuous, though abused in life
Is purified in Godly affection

Virtue swallows up virginity
Washes that soiled in time

Makes pure that once defiled
Transforms base desire into holy hope

Virginity without virtue
Is death waiting to be born

Virtue without virginity
Flourishes as a healing balm

It is the victory over our shame
And freedom from our curse

Virtue is the purity
To which virginity only points

August 1996

11.

HE ENTERED MY PAIN

I cried unto the Lord
He did not answer
With all my heart I sought His face
He would not speak

Where have You gone
Mighty Lord of Israel?
Where have you hidden Your Presence
He whose eye is on the sparrow?

Why have you forsaken me
Abandoned me in my misery?
Why are You not moved
By the feeling of my infirmity?

My sorrow engulfs me
My anguish cries out
In torment I shout
With passion I plea

In vain I dreamed I might please You
Find favor in Your sight
In joy I would have served You
In the shadow of Your might

My enemies would destroy me
They devour my flesh
Their arrows pierce my soul
Assaulting from within and without

Gone are my hopes and dreams
My armor stolen in the night
Dignity, valor, righteousness
Pilfered in my distress

I cried out for my deliverer
He could not – would not – come
Delayed by what? Distracted by whom?
Then silent before my tomb

Yet will I serve Him
He will not abandon me to this pit
He will breathe life into these bones
Shelter me beneath His throne

He is alpha and omega
Beginning and end
More faithful than a brother
Already a proven friend

He did hear my cry
With certainty He responded
But I did not have ears
With which to hear

He saw my sorrow
Felt my wounds
I could not see, but He came
And entered my pain.

I cannot see tomorrow
Cannot hope for gain
For now it is enough
He entered my pain

"I can," "I will," "I should," "I must"
Words that drove me to this grave
Words of promise
Lacking power to save

"Though He himself should slay me,"
To these words I choose to cling
"In Him alone I trust
He alone my King."

February 2001

12.

I WILL BLESS THE LORD AT ALL TIMES

I will bless Him when the sun rises
I will bless Him when the sun sets
I will bless Him in the noon hour
I will bless Him in the midnight hour
I will bless Him in the daylight
I will bless Him in the darkest night
I will Bless Him on the mountain top
I will bless Him in the valley below
I will bless Him when the spring blossoms bright
I will bless him in winter's frigid white
I will bless Him when I am young
I will bless Him when I am old
I will bless Him when I am strong
I will bless Him when I am weak

I will bless Him when all is well
I will bless Him when troubles assail
I will bless Him when others speak well of me
I will bless Him when others disdain my name
I will bless Him in the season of plenty
I will bless Him in times of want
I will bless Him in the day of birth
I will bless Him in the hour of death
I will bless the Lord!
At All Times, I Will Bless His Name!

November 2001

13

FOR SUCH A TIME AS THIS

I will not despair
I will hope in God
I will remember His blessings
I will rejoice in his goodness
I will take comfort in His presence
I will draw strength from His Word
I will live for His glory
I will do His will
I will rise up and bless His Name
I Have Been Born for Such a Time as This!

November 2001

"Joined in heart, mind, and spirit for all time."
Bachlott Cemetery
Brantley County, Georgia

14.

LOVE

Love is a fleeting dream
A phantom it would seem
Oh, yes, it is real
Causes the soul to know, to feel

But love can never be contained
It moves as it wills without refrain
Captivating our thoughts
Giving new meaning to the words "I ought"

Love focuses all our hope
Broadens our horizon's scope
Demands our life center in another
Rejects the attention of all others

Love makes the world so clear
Drives away all our fears
Love is an inner gyroscope
The sustainer of our deepest hope

Love is a balancing bar
A navigator's guiding star
Love demands our full attention
Fuels a singular devotion

Love allows for no chance
Of forbidden romance
Love refuses to entertain
Lust, hidden desires, by any name

Love is a fickle friend,
Yet, faithful to the end
An invisible master
Pushing forward ever faster

Giving color to the flowers
And songs to the birds
It causes the sun to shine brighter
Our spirits to soar ever higher

Yet, it also takes our hand
Leads through darker lands
Forces us to face our fears
Recalls the sorrows of our years

Breaks and tears our very being
Always contending
Unable to rest,
or to give rest

Never satisfied
Till both have died
Or each is whole
and the two are one.

March 2008

Corinth Primitive Baptist Church
Charlton County, Georgia

15.

MAKE YOUR REDEMPTION COMPLETE

Father,
You hold all things together
You make all things new
Your redemption is perfect
Purchased out of death
Unto life, abundant life
Our destiny is purity and perfection
Not a static state of endless protection
Rather, a dynamic embrace of all we have known
And all that is yet to be shown

Yet I scarce believe you will transform
My brokenness into wholeness
My pain into pleasure
My sorrow into joy
Betrayal into fidelity
Evil into good

Can these dry bones live?
Can they be transfigured?
Can they join the pulse
Of Your pure heart?
Contain the flow
Of Your boundless love?
Can they endure the glory
Of Your consuming face?
Can they survive the power
Of Your holy embrace?
Can they ever grasp the beauty
Of Your matchless grace?
Can they know
As they are known?

Will all things be made new?
Will my memories remain
And yet be changed?
Can these thoughts
Enjoy transubstantiation?
Can all that I am
All I have known
Be engulfed in Your beauty?
What grace must you apply
To the emptiness of my being
That I might fit
Into the fullness of Your image?

Let every thought
Be imprisoned to Your Majesty
Every recollection
Made factual and true
Every betrayal
A revelation of Your fidelity
Every pain
A song of Your goodness
Every disappointment
A hymn to Your faithfulness
Every threat of death
A proclamation of Your life

Let every fiber of my being
From the time you wove me together
In my mother's womb
Through every breath I have drawn
Every joy and every sorrow
Past, present, and for all tomorrows
For as long as I am
Proclaim boldly Your greatness
Your faithfulness
Your beauty
And Your mercy

Savior,
At your appearance
May I sing in harmony
With the symphony
Of Your creation?
Breathed upon by your Spirit
May I dance that flawless dance
Of the redeemed
Moving in the splendor
Of Your presence?

In that day
When all that is gives You glory
Martyrs and saints singing your praise
Angels continuing their ancient anthem
Flowers, plants and trees
Joining in the revelry
The crown of thorns
now a royal diadem
The cross unfolded
Bejeweled as your throne

In that day
All creation will your name revere
Every nation bowing every knee
The pit too will sing
Of the beauty of Your holy mountain
Hell itself will then proclaim
The righteousness of Your reign
And the splendor of Your Name
Judgment will your grace reveal
As the peoples gather to be healed.

The damned will bear witness
To Your mercy
In Your presence
Consumed by Your absence
Touched by Your love without end
Unknowing but revealing
The greatness of Your plan.

And so we plea
Come quickly Lord Jesus
Fill all things with Your presence
Make all things new
Make Your Redemption Complete!

February 2009

16.

CONSIDER CREATION

Consider now creation
In its whole and in each part
Every photon, neuron, and function
God revealed in His art

His glory frames the horizons
His beauty adorns each flower
His majesty cloaks the heavens
The eternal imbues every hour

All creatures by Him adorned
Each kissed by the breath of God
Humans alone in His image formed
The Creator impressed on sod

Each day a sculpture
Shaped by the finger of God
Each moment a monument
To His creative power

January 2011

17.

INTO YOUR PRESENCE

In the cool of the day
I run into Your presence
In the garden of Your Word
Hungry for Your touch, Your face
Your will, Your warm embrace
There I quiet my spirit
And listen for Your voice
Echoing through those ancient books
Scribed by human hands
Both eternal and created
Word of God born in thoughts of men

More than a window into the heavens
Or a relic of the past
The Spirit hums across the pages
Grace and Truth for all the ages
Love beyond imagination
Wed to human communication
Mysteries hidden from the angels
Written in the lyrics of mere mortals
In the whole and in each part
Intoning Your very heart
Every syllable a revelation
Alpha and Omega within creation

October 2011

18.

THE ATONEMENT

He stepped out of His glory
And wrapped Himself in darkness
The Creator became the created
The Eternal conceived as mortal
He who knew no sin, became sin
For our sakes, love, grace and truth
Embraced all our bitterness
Bound up our brokenness
And healed all our diseases

Some would limit the atonement
In its history and in its effect
To the cross as seat of judgment
And the predestined elect
They would bury our transgressions
In a moment of confessions
And His foreknown pronouncement
The chosen decreed as innocent

But His propitiation
Brackets the incarnation
Fully God and fully man
Salvation without end
And its effect on all creation
Every tribe, every nation
The claim of His grace
Rests on all the human race

Yes, our sentence was commuted
His righteousness imputed
But His purpose was much greater
Full communion with our Creator
With pardon came renewal
Freedom from sin's rule
Yes, full redemption
Holiness imparted
Entire sanctification
A new order of creation

November 2011

19.

PRAYERS OF MY YOUTH

In my youth I prayed
"Lord, break me
Melt me
Mold me
And shape me
Make me into all you want me to be
I am the least of your kingdom
But surely you can use me
Search me and know me
Cleanse me
Purify my soul
Burn out the dross
Purge me with hyssop
Somehow make me whole
A vessel of Your glory and Your honor
Make me fit for your kingdom
If worthy only of the shadow of Your passing
Help me serve you
That's all I ask"

Little did I know
The path I would walk
How excited prayers for perfection
Could morph into pleas for protection
I had assumed it all quick and simple
Death, new life, certainty and direction
Infused in but a moment
All He would require
Was sincerity in surrender
Instead, I found my Father
More patient than I
More willing to suffer with me
Than I with Him
I could not know the cost of my quest
The anvils of my breaking
The furnaces of my undoing
The presses of my forming

Neither could I know
Brokenness would not expose
The purity I had imagined
In the crevices of my soul
Grew leaven unknown
Stains thought under the blood
Surfaced in the light of His Word
How could I know
Melting is slow
Dross lingers long
Dreams of valor vanish
Hope for survival would seem enough
Bold prayers of surrender
Become pleas for a defender
Then desperate cries for a deliverer
"Jesus of Nazareth,
Thou Son of David,
Have mercy on me.
Help me! Help me!
Help me, if You can."

I did not know His hammer and His anvil
Would be persons whom I knew
Disappointments and betrayal
His smelting pot
The altar of service
Ministry in His Name

If I knew then
What I know now
Would I pray the same?
Would I plead the glory of His Name?
Would I offer
"All that I am,
All that I have,
All I hope to be.
They are Yours, Oh Lord.
Not my will
But Thine be done?"

Yes, moving now from the summer
To the autumn of my life
Considering all that has gone before
I cannot but pray
"Whatever it takes,
Break me, melt me, mold me,
Make me into all
You created me to be.
Until I find
My rest in Thee.
Help me serve you.
Hear my plea.
That is all I ask."

April 2009

ABOUT THE AUTHOR

Jackie David Johns, Ph.D., and his wife, Cheryl Bridges Johns, have served as co-pastors of the New Covenant Church of God (Cleveland, Tennessee) since January of 1989.

He is Professor of Discipleship and Christian Formation at the Pentecostal Theological Seminary where he has taught since 1985.

All photographs by

Jackie David Johns

Cover photograph

Okefenokee Swamp

Charlton County, Georgia

www.ingramcontent.com/pod-product-compliance
Lightning Source LLC
Chambersburg PA
CBHW071021040426
42443CB00007B/891

* 9 7 8 0 6 1 5 5 7 0 6 4 8 *